YOUR LIFE IS A GIFT

So Make the Most of It!

Ken Keyes, Jr.

with Penny Keyes

Illustrated by Ann Hauser

Second Edition

A Revision of
How to Make Your Life Work or
Why Aren't You Happy?
by Ken Keyes, Jr. and
Tolly Burkan

LOVE LINE BOOKS
Coos Bay, Oregon 97420

Your purchase of any Love Line book helps to build a more loving and caring world. Royalties are used by a nonprofit organization dedicated to teaching Living Love and the Science of Happiness.

Your Life is a Gift may be obtained through your local bookstore, or you may order it from Love Line Books, 700 Commercial Ave., Coos Bay, OR 97420 for $8.95 plus $3.00 for shipping and handling. See pages 201 to 209 for information about Ken's other life-enriching books.

The Twelve Pathways, the drawings, or up to 10 pages of this book may be freely quoted or reprinted without permission provided credit is given in the following form:

© **1987 by Living Love Publications**

First Edition published In 1974
Second Edition published In 1987
Total In Print 185,000 copies

Printed on acid-free paper for permanency

Library of Congress Cataloging-In-Publication Data

Keyes, Ken.
    Your life is a gift.
    Rev. ed. of: How to make your life work, or,
Why aren't you happy?
    1. Happiness.   2. Consciousness.   3. Success.
I. Keyes, Ken. How to make your life work, or, Why
aren't you happy? II. Title.
BF575.H27K49   1987   158'.1   86-21385
ISBN 0-915972-12-3 (pbk.) (alk. paper)

LOVE LINE BOOKS

700 Commercial Avenue, Coos Bay, OR 97420

**Dedicated with love to
HILDA CHARLTON
who has given her life, love,
and light to everyone.**

**Are you
making the most
of your life?**

When you are given a gift,
it often comes with directions.

A stereo comes with an instruction book;
a car with an operator's manual.

Your life is a gift.

Would you like to know how to make
your life work?

WE MEAN REALLY WORK WELL?

Cut out anxiety, anger, fear, jealousy,
irritation, resentment, boredom, suffering . . .
unhappiness . . . . ?

You don't think it's possible, do you?

HA!

It's just because you were never given
the directions on how to do it.

9

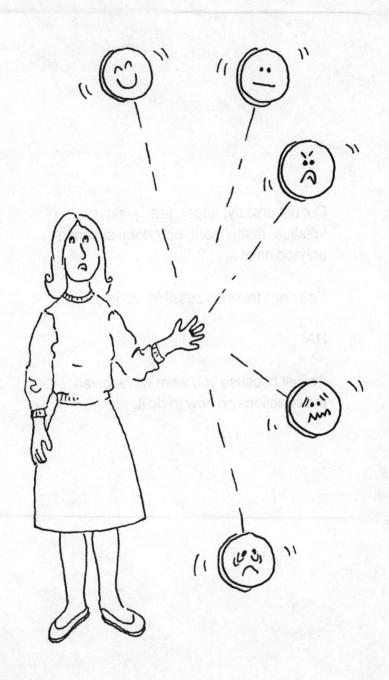

Your first step in learning how to do it
is to realize that the basic way you now try
to improve your life will ALWAYS keep you
bouncing like a yo-yo between happiness
and unhappiness.

If you are not CONSISTENTLY HAPPY,
it means that you are stumbling through life
and not taking full advantage of your potential
which has been inside you—
just waiting to be developed.

How many people
do you know who feel
CONSISTENTLY HAPPY?

We know you try hard.

We know you're a good person.
(We hope you know that, too.)

So what's wrong?

People who feel unhappy don't know
why they feel unhappy . . . .

If they knew why unhappiness happens,
they would start correcting the situation
so they could feel happy . . . .

BUT THEY DON'T . . .
BECAUSE THEY DON'T KNOW
WHAT **CAUSES** UNHAPPINESS.

The CAUSE of unhappiness is not a mystery . . .

It's actually quite simple.

Since you have read this far,
perhaps you are now ready
to study the cause of unhappiness—
ALL unhappiness—
so you can get on with
feeling happy more of the time.

Remember, this approach can work
even in situations that in the past
seemed to cause miserable feelings
(sickness, money shortage, calamity,
visiting relatives, divorce, etc., etc., etc.).

Ready?

It will sound so simple
that you may dismiss it
all too quickly—
without really understanding
how it applies
to the very special conditions
of your particular life.

BUT DOING IT IS NOT SO SIMPLE . . . .

IT TAKES A STRONG MAN
OR A STRONG WOMAN.

Here it is.

You have MENTAL HABITS
that AUTOMATICALLY trigger feelings
of unhappiness
when people and situations around you
DO NOT FIT YOUR EXPECTATIONS.

In other words,
YOUR EXPECTATIONS
create your unhappiness.

It's your emotion-backed demands
that make you suffer—
it's not the world,
the people around you,
or even you YOURSELF!

Let's call these demands and expectations **"ADDICTIVE DEMANDS."**

An **ADDICTIVE DEMAND** is any emotion-backed thought that says something must be a certain way for you to feel happy, secure, or satisfied. It is a desire conditioned into your mind or body which, if not satisfied, AUTOMATICALLY triggers a separating emotion: fear, anger, jealousy, anxiety, frustration, irritation, resentment, sadness, disgust, hate, etc., etc., etc.

You don't experience an unpleasant, separating emotion that . . . if prolonged results in unhappiness . . .
UNLESS
a life event is triggering
one or more of your addictive demands.

THUS, YOUR ADDICTIVE DEMANDS ARE THE **SOLE** CAUSE OF YOUR UNHAPPINESS!!!

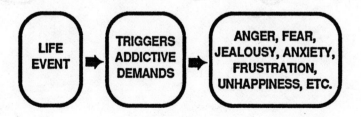

LIFE EVENT → TRIGGERS ADDICTIVE DEMANDS → ANGER, FEAR, JEALOUSY, ANXIETY, FRUSTRATION, UNHAPPINESS, ETC.

Where did you learn
that you must act like a robot
by automatically triggering upset
if a life event
doesn't fit your inner programming?

Are you going to let the world
and the people around you
TRIGGER ADDICTIVE DEMANDS
and thus control your inner experience?

Why do you let your happiness
depend on people
and happenings around you?

The outside world of life events
can never MAKE you unhappy . . . .

Only YOU
can create your unhappiness—
or your happiness.

For example . . . .

You really don't have to allow
YOUR MENTAL HABITS
to REJECT YOU
if someone criticizes you.

You don't have to allow
YOUR MENTAL HABITS
to MAKE YOU UPSET
if the people you are with
don't do what they promised.

There's no law that requires you to let
YOUR MIND
addictively demand anything—
which thereby TRIGGERS
in a robot-like way
the EMOTIONS of fear, frustration, and anger.

You've probably been spending
most of your time and energy
either feeling like a victim
or trying to manipulate yourself,
other people, and situations
in order to feel happy.

Well . . . has it worked?

Do you feel happy MOST OF THE TIME?

Have you ever succeeded in
CONTROLLING THE WORLD
(yourself, other people, and situations)
to such a degree
that you felt really satisfied
for even a month?

Through your own personal growth,
would you like to
relax the fussing in your head
and feel happy
more and more of the time?

Your ego/mind
tells you that people are
DOING IT to you.

But you are really allowing
your PROGRAMMING
to do it to you!

When you get into a system called Living Love,
you learn that there are:
- (1) LIFE EVENTS, and there are
- (2) your INSIDE PROGRAMMINGS
      that determine your
      RESPONSES TO THE LIFE EVENTS.

You know how life is—
you "win" some and you "lose" some.

You think you "lose" when you don't get
what you addictively want—
or you do get what you addictively don't want.

With addictive programming, life events
can trigger fear, frustration, and anger
which if perpetuated result in unhappiness.

You can actually retrain
your biocomputer (your mind)
so that it will NOT automatically trigger
addictive demands.

Perhaps no one ever fully explained to you
how you can use your marvelous biocomputer
to do its job properly . . . .

After all, every computer
requires a skilled operator
to make the best use
of all the wonderful things it can do.

We're glad you now have
an operator's manual.

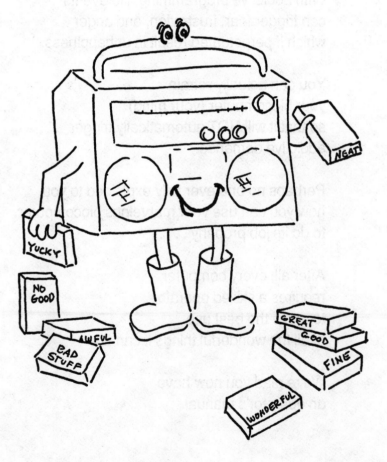

If you put a program into a computer
and it doesn't work well,
you don't berate the computer.

You just set your mind on acquiring
a new program
that operates the way you want it to.

If you put a cassette program
into your tape player
and what comes out sounds awful to you,
you don't criticize the tape player.

You do something about
the program on the cassette.

Are you aware of the programs—
mental habits, conditioning—
that you've put in your head
since even before you were born?

When something in your life
doesn't go the way you want it to,
do you blame yourself (computer, tape player)
or do you blame the unskillful program
that you picked up sometime in the past?

Just remember that
YOU ARE NOT YOUR PROGRAMMING.
Members of your family
are not their programming.
Your friends are not their programming.
Your enemies are not their programming.

Let's focus on helping ourselves
change the unskillful programming
that slows us down
like barnacles on the bottom of a ship.

Let's be careful not to blame the ship
when it's the barnacles
that are causing the problems.
Just as we can remove the barnacles,
we can do something
to change our programming
that will give us
new responses to life situations.

Each new day
can be an interesting adventure.
So let's learn
how to enjoy every new day!

The society in which you were raised
led you to believe
that you could "win" enough
to live a happy life if you had:
more money . . .
or more prestige . . .
or more power . . .
or more free time . . .
or more sex . . .
or more "stuff" that you can buy in stores . . .
more, more, more!

YOU REALLY ACCUMULATED
A LOT OF "STUFF,"
DIDN'T YOU?

So, do you feel happy?
CONSISTENTLY?
Are you really in love with living?
Are you in love with
the prospect of facing
each and every new day
of your life?

Do you feel that your life is a gift?

You've kept yourself in a tizzy
trying to make it in life
by getting people and situations
to fit your inner addictive programs
of security (approval, money, etc.),
sensation (comfort, pleasures, etc.),
and power (pride, prestige,
skill in controlling, etc.).

My, how you've tried!

The demanding way
in which you have been trying
to solve one problem in your life
usually creates
the next problem in your life.

Lonely?
Your rational mind might suggest
that you need more money
so that you can attract the people
you want in your life.

You switch to a better paying job!

Now you may have added business worries . . . .

So your business worries keep you from
relaxing and enjoying your friends . . . .

Do you have an ulcer yet?

When you work hard to acquire
"something" to make you happy—
AND YOU GET IT—
do you then worry about
losing it or damaging it?

Will it ever become obsolete?

Wouldn't you like another one?

. . . a bigger one? . . . a better one?

Do you really want to know
how to get the world outside your head
to harmonize
with the world inside your head
(your programming)?

EMOTIONAL

ACCEPTANCE

It's so simple.

INSTEAD OF WEARING YOURSELF OUT
TRYING TO CHANGE THE PEOPLE
AND SITUATIONS IN YOUR LIFE,
GIVE YOURSELF THE OPTION
TO CONCENTRATE ON CHANGING
YOUR **ADDICTIVE DEMANDS** . . .
YOUR REQUIREMENTS AND EXPECTATIONS—
YOUR "ABSOLUTE NECESSITIES" . . . .

THIS IS THE **ONLY WAY**
TO **CONSISTENTLY**
GET THE OUTSIDE AND THE INSIDE
TO HARMONIZE TOGETHER.
THE STRATEGY IS SIMPLE.
WHEN YOU CAN'T CHANGE
THE LIFE EVENTS AROUND YOU,
YOU CAN QUICKLY SHIFT GEARS
AND CHANGE YOUR PROGRAMMING!

It is impossible
to have enough money or power
(or cleverness or sympathy)
to change the outside world
to consistently fit your inner demands.
Even billionaires and emperors
never succeeded
in finding happiness
by changing the world.

Look at Napoleon.

Look at Hitler.

They couldn't do it.
They tried like no one else in history,
and they still couldn't do it.

The outside world
can never give you "enough"
if you are programmed
to keep on demanding things
you don't already have
or more of what you do have.

If you always want "more"
you will never have "enough."

As you let go of your addictive demands,
YOU CAN STILL HAVE PREFERENCES!
You can prefer that something
happen a certain way,
but if it doesn't happen,
you can remain happy—
because it is not a condition
for your happiness.

With a **PREFERENCE**:
1. You can still want what you want.
2. You can still try to make changes.
3. You can still think you're right.
4. You can more skillfully achieve your
   desired internal experience.
5. You just don't have to feel upset
   or unhappy!

If it DOES happen the way you want . . . FINE!

If it doesn't, you're not hung up.

The game is to set things up in your head
so that either way,
YOU CAN'T LOSE!

It never occurs to most people
that this simple solution
can work so well!

Let's view all this with a little perspective.

Isn't it easier to change your programming than to keep changing people and situations to fit your separate-self programming?

Your requirements and expectations?

Your **ADDICTIVE DEMANDS**?!?

Here are your choices:

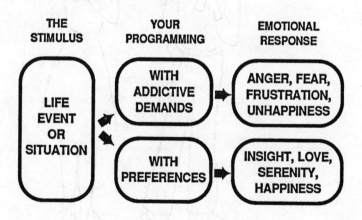

THE STIMULUS	YOUR PROGRAMMING	EMOTIONAL RESPONSE
LIFE EVENT OR SITUATION	WITH ADDICTIVE DEMANDS ➡	ANGER, FEAR, FRUSTRATION, UNHAPPINESS
	WITH PREFERENCES ➡	INSIGHT, LOVE, SERENITY, HAPPINESS

"But can't I ever try
to change the outside world?"

SURE!

Just use LOVING COMMUNICATION
that comes from
your unified-self programming. . .
which means not being **addicted**
to people or things changing.

If they can flow with your
gentle, loving communication,
then you can change people and situations
in a way that does not have
any backlash
to create unhappiness in your life.

Make your loving communication
in a manner which indicates
that you emotionally accept
AND LOVE THEM UNCONDITIONALLY—
regardless of whether
they do what you prefer.

Depending on their programming,
they will less likely experience
any kind of pressure from you . . .
either gross or subtle.

With all but saints,
trying to change people
by withdrawing your love
or by power tripping
if they don't do what you want
tends to kill love in their hearts.

And if your loving communication
does not produce change—
you still remain happy
because you are not addicted
to the results of your actions.

You view life as a game
and are not obsessed
with winning or losing—
you simply enjoy playing.

If you're not addicted to "winning,"
there is no way you can ever create
the experience of loss—
you just enjoy the game.

SEPARATE-SELF PROGRAMMING

UNIFIED-SELF PROGRAMMING

Our demanding programming
makes us feel separate and alienated
from ourselves and others
when life events
don't go the way we want.

We call this "separate-self programming."

When addictive demands
are upleveled to preferences,
we feel a unity with ourselves and others
even when things aren't the way
we want them to be.

We call this "unified-self programming"
for it enables us to feel in harmony
with life conditons around us—
and we can still want to change things
and can certainly try to do so.

EMOTIONAL
ACCEPTANCE

Higher consciousness
calls for emotional flexibility.

You become a master
at emotionally accepting
what was previously unacceptable.

Emotional acceptance
does not necessarily mean
that you have to go on someone else's trip
in your journey of life.

It just means
that you don't make yourself upset with them . . .
no matter what they say or do.

You realize that you can emotionally accept them
as they live out their programming—
even though you may not want to be involved
in living that way yourself.

So now you know what's needed
to make your life work more smoothly.

Unconditional love . . . emotional acceptance . . .
brings harmony to your life.

Instead of continually striving
and fighting life events
to change and manipulate them
to fit your inner programming,
you just learn
to be mentally and emotionally flexible.

You master the techniques
for changing your inside programming—
upleveling addictive demands to preferences—
so that you don't drive yourself wild
when life doesn't fit your programmed models
of how it all should be.

There are no "shoulds" or "shouldn'ts"
as far as existing events are concerned.

They are the way they are . . . here and now!

Don't waste your energy
regretting what is here and now . . .
running emotion-backed thoughts
that things SHOULD be different.

Only your programming creates
"shoulds" and "shouldn'ts" . . . .

In reality, they do not exist.

If you wish to involve yourself
in trying to modify a situation,
preferably from a nondemanding space,
remember that you are doing it simply
because that is your role
in the GAME of life.

You may often choose to play the game
of changing yourself or others—
or the conditions around you.

Your programming called "social conscience"
will often prefer
to make great changes.

Just play the game of change
understandingly,
compassionately,
lovingly.

Thus,
instead of spending the rest of your life
struggling to keep the world in line
with your expectations and demands,
you modify your programming.

As you gradually increase your skill
in upleveling addictive demands to preferences,
a miraculous thing happens!

You learn to love more and demand less.

And then . . . like magic,

THE WORLD FEELS GREAT!

And you may now have
even more physical energy
for playing the game
of changing things.

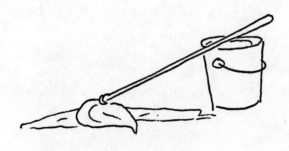

Can it really be that simple?

Well, when you try it
you will see for yourself.

93

The past is nonexistent
and the future is imaginary.

The more your thoughts dwell on the past
or on the future,
the more you'll miss
the precious opportunities
to enjoy your life
and to learn new things
in the here and now.

Today is perfect—
perfect for your enjoyment
OR YOUR GROWTH!

It is a day which you can enjoy . . .
unless you are demandingly comparing it
with the dead past
or the imagined future—
neither of which really exists now.

As long as you are
feeling unhappy with what **is**,
solely because it does not fit
the program in your head,
you are going to make yourself feel
miserable or dissatisfied.

You have got to enjoy "BEING"
and stop worrying about "BECOMING"
because there is no end
to what you can worry about . . . .

Your life will **never** seem fulfilled
until your programming
can let you feel happy
here and now.

Yesterday is over.
Enjoy the memories.
Learn what you can from it
and lovingly let it go.

"Tomorrow" always becomes "today."

It's fine to make plans.
But if you keep looking
anxiously ahead into "tomorrows,"
when they become "todays"
you will still not enjoy them
because you will be preoccupied
with dreams and worries
about "new" tomorrows.

Don't spend your life missing today . . .
waiting for the day your programming
CAN LET YOU FEEL HAPPY.

If you don't feel happy TODAY,
what dramatic difference will come
with tomorrow—
especially if the programming you use now
is precisely what produced the "today"
that you're unhappy with?

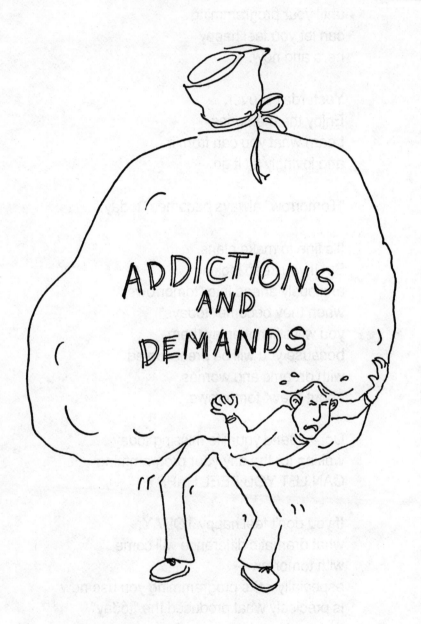

If your big, crushing bag of addictions
and demands doesn't get smaller . . .
your life will never work optimally.

Fulfillment and inner peace
will elude you . . . .

When will you realize
that "today" IS the "tomorrow"
you hoped for "yesterday"?

So why waste it looking for new tomorrows—
ENJOY IT NOW
because it's already yours.

The cycle of dissatisfaction will continue
unless YOU stop it . . . .

How about TODAY?

Whenever your mind is preoccupied
with the rut of "pasting" or "futuring"—
and your demands are making you reject
the here and now situation in your life—
and you get upset and start to worry,
you are depriving yourself of:

1. **ENERGY.** You waste energy when you worry
   about the past or future. Internally rejecting
   and demanding wears you out.

2. **INSIGHT.** You may be sure that your insight is at
   a low point. When you are upset, all you see
   with any central awareness is what you fear
   or what you desire. The actions (or nonactions)
   that offer the optimal solutions to your problem
   will occur to you only when you are cooled out
   and can see the entire situation with perspective.

3. **LOVE.** When you are caught in the grip of
   anger, jealousy, anxiety, or resentment,
   you are probably making yourself feel alienated
   from people around you and are throwing someone
   out of your heart. You may be turning away from
   the people who would otherwise be helpful to you.

An individual who operates with his or her
unified-self programming understands
that the misery other people are experiencing
is caused by their addictive demands.

When we operate with our separate-self
programming, we seem stuck in thinking that
the cause of our misery is anything but
our addictive programming.

So often we think the people we're involved with
are causing us to feel unhappy,
and we decide that the world around us
is pretty rotten.

When we respond to the people and situations in
our lives in critical, separating, unloving ways,
we tend to attract and create even more of what
we don't want.

This makes us feel even more upset
and now we are really sure
that the world is at fault.

We continue spiraling downward
to create tons of suffering
and unhappiness in our lives.

The more deeply we understand
that our demanding programming
is the actual cause of our unhappiness,
the more determined we can become
to do something about that cause.

We begin to generate
happiness and satisfaction in our lives
when we steadily free ourselves
from our own addictive traps.

So now you have to make a decision—

Do you want to continue burdening yourself
for the rest of your life
with an enormous load of addictions . . .
emotion-backed demands, rigid expectations,
fixed ideas of how the world SHOULD be,
emotional models of how people SHOULD treat you,
etc., etc., etc.?

Remember—
YOU put this addictive programming
into your head.

Most of your security, sensation, and power
addictions were programmed by you
during the first few years of your life
when your biocomputer was immature
and you were completely at the mercy
of outside influences.

What you experienced and programmed then
still determines many of your reactions
to the world today.

You are not your programming—
just as a computer
is not its programming . . . .

When you change the programming,
the computer remains the same,
but it OPERATES differently.

Dump your addictions!

Addictive programs
keep you from living the happiest,
most effective life you can.

You are a success because you're alive rig

You've made it!

Most of what you struggle with
are the games of life—
your soap opera—
your personal drama.

You were born with
a few addictive programmings . . .
mainly some simple survival demands involving
food, air, and protection from physical harm.

If you are not involved in meeting needs
concerned with immediate physical survival,
and you find that you feel upset about something,
you are suffering from the "disease of demanding."

Why be ADDICTED to something
which is not needed for survival?

ALL OTHER
EMOTION-BACKED DEMANDS
ARE SICKNESS!

There's a lot of sickness around, isn't there?

You can heal yourself.

Another way of looking
at this predicament
is that our social epidemic
of addictive demands
is keeping each of us locked up
in a self-maintained jail cell.

Some of us
are learning to free ourselves
from the jail that is created
by our programming
and perpetuated by the involvement
of our egos and rational minds.

ARE YOU READY for the jailbreak?

Are you strong enough
for the dash to freedom?

Until you realize that you have nothing to lose
but your unhappiness,
you won't be able to break free
from the tyranny
of your addictive programming . . . .

You'll just keep churning
with thoughts and feelings
that make you reject
what is here and now
in your life.

You must realize that
you can never make it in life
by trying only to control others.

In many life situations
it's a thousand times more practical
to be in control of your own programming.

CONTROLLING YOUR PROGRAMMING
REALLY WORKS . . .
IF YOU HAVE THE GUTS TO DO IT.

Controlling your programming
does not mean
that you repress your feelings.

That is ulcerville.

To live an increasingly effective,
peaceful, and happy life,
you must reprogram your biocomputer
so that it does not kick in
emotionally separating REACTIONS
to the SITUATIONS around you.

As you begin
to reprogram the tapes in your head,
you will eliminate the causes
of fear, frustration, and anger . . .
which you may have been repressing.

You can now remain tuned-in,
centered, and loving.

ADDICTION

PREFERENCE

Ready to do it?

Okay, let's go.

The game is to begin to let go
of your addictive demands . . .
to uplevel your addictions
to "preferences."

You will recall that an **ADDICTION**
is any demand or expectation that you place
upon yourself, another person,
or a situation in your life
which can AUTOMATICALLY trigger
separating emotions, such as
worry, dread, disgust, boredom, impatience,
resentment, hostility, and annoyance . . . .

A PREFERENCE is a desire that doesn't make
you feel upset or unhappy if it isn't met.

For example, your programming could
addictively demand that your friend show up
at a designated time—or it could PREFER that—
in which case you wouldn't feel upset
if your friend showed up late.

Wouldn't you rather your friends
have such preferential programming
when you're late?

ADDICTION

PREFERENCE

When your programming
is a parade of preferences,
you can enjoy your here and now consistently.

When you, other people, and situations
do not fit your programmed preferences,
it's still okay.

You simply make an emotionally accepting,
loving communication which says,
"I love you unconditionally.
Even though I may want you to act differently,
it doesn't matter to my heart
whether or not
you fit my preferences."

When you, other people, and situations
happen to fit your preferences,
you are able to trigger feelings of joy,
increased love, appreciation, and happiness.

You lose only what you never wanted
when you uplevel addictions to preferences—
YOUR UNHAPPINESS!

ADDICTION

PREFERENCE

When your biocomputer
is largely free from addictive programming
and you're using preferential programming,
YOU CREATE the experience
of living in A WONDERFUL WORLD.

You may have lots of models
of how you want things to be,
and yet you aren't addicted
to getting them met.

Things are the way they are
and you remain happy.

And you can still play the preferential game
of trying to change things.

THIS IS HOW TO ENJOY
THE GIFT
OF YOUR LIFE!

It's fine to "prefer" money, approval,
sex, comfort, or anything—
but don't kid yourself
into thinking it's a "preference"
if it is really an addiction.

It is quite easy to tell them apart . . . .

Will you feel frustrated or disappointed
if you actually do not get
the money, approval, sex, comfort, etc.
that you said you "preferred"?

Hm-m-m-m-m-m-m.
Remember,
only ADDICTIONS cause unhappiness.

It doesn't appear that you are yet convinced.

What are you saying?

Are you saying that if you don't get mad,
anxious, or jealous when people treat you
a certain way, they'll just run over you as if
you were a doormat?

Or are you afraid that if you
eliminate fear from your biocomputer,
you may get hurt in certain situations?

Are you wondering whether
separating emotions have a real place in life
to help you avoid pain
and gradually mold people and situations
so you can live with them comfortably?

You've got an interesting point there.

If you don't respond at all to the world, the world will probably just roll over you, because it won't see you. People won't know what you want . . . because they aren't mind readers.

But the problem with using separating emotions to manipulate and control the world is that they only work to a certain point. They will never enable you to control and dominate people and situations ENOUGH to give you the experience of feeling secure, to give you what seems like enough enjoyable sensations, and to give you a sense of enough effectiveness and power in your life.

Sure, if you competently manipulate, you will have more security, sensations, and power than if you made no attempt at all to interact with the world. But your addictions will keep you trotting along like a donkey chasing a carrot which is dangling from a stick tied around its neck. Every now and then you may get a nibble of the carrot if it swings your way, BUT YOU'LL NEVER GET THE WHOLE CARROT.

You may have moments of pleasure, but remember, if you develop skill in using this "operator's manual,"
you can CONSISTENTLY experience happiness . .

HMPF!

"What if I'm being attacked
or am in physical danger?"

Well, chances are pretty good that if you panic
or get excited or become emotionally upset
you will not be able to think clearly and
you might even act in a way that will actually
contribute to being injured.

If you stay centered and loving in **all** situations,
you will be assured of acting from a clear perspective and you will automatically react in a way
that will produce the BEST POSSIBLE results.

HAVE YOU EVER **IMPROVED**
YOUR PERFORMANCE BY WORRYING
or by feeling unhappy
because your programming is resisting
a here-and-now situation?

You actually are more secure
(financially and otherwise)
when you uplevel addictive demands to preferences,
simply because you are not impeded
by the handicap of worry and frustration
which distorts your perception
and also prevents you from enjoying **every** aspect
of your business and personal life.

Remember, you are not trying to change
what you are doing . . .
only the programming that determines
your internal experience.

The game is to move toward
DOING EVERYTHING
from a balanced and compassionate position
that you access inside you.

As you increase your skill
in flowing with life
and use "loving communication"
for implementing change,
miracles begin to happen in your life.

You begin to pull away
from the separate-self
"me-vs.-you" force field
you've been creating.

You begin to live
in a unified-self
"me-and-you" experience.

You begin to perceive life
as your friend—
not your adversary.

You appreciate the gift of your life.

Reacting with a separating emotion
won't help you get the best possible results.

When you uplevel an addiction to a preference,
you clear your head
and put things in their proper perspective.

Sure, if the roof leaks,
you can INTELLECTUALLY see the situation
as being one which needs improving . . .
and you can EMOTIONALLY accept it
as part of the here and now.

Then you can do
what your integrated head and heart
tell you to do—fix the roof.

When you use preferential programming
to stay cool, calm, and collected,
you'll be able to respond
in an optimal way.

Sounds like magic, doesn't it?

It's the magic
of insight and love.

It may sound crazy . . . but it actually works.

This is not a theory, it is an observable fact.

And it's a system which has proven itself
over thousands of years.

When you give it all up (inside),
you get it all back (outside or inside).

What you give up
is your emotional attachment
to a rock-like set
of security, sensation, and power demands.

What you get back
is a relaxed, loving, friendly world
that does so much
to love and serve you in return.

Everyone that earnestly applies this approach
experiences a more enjoyable and effective life.

And now you know what to do!

When you are the slave of addictive programming, your ego constantly filters and rewrites the incoming sensory data. Your rational mind reflects a distorted version of the world . . . one which is biased toward perceiving a lack of enough security, sensation, or power in your life. Because your separate-self programming is being used, your biocomputer operates in a way that shortchanges you, confuses you, misleads you— and prevents your life from working properly. You see things through the distorting filter of your demanding programming.

When you uplevel many of your addictions to preferences, you will discover that your body may not need as much sleep as you now require. Plus, you will have much more energy during your waking hours. You'll find that your addictions were causing the stress and struggle in your life and making you needlessly expend tons of energy.

You will begin to increase your insight and perceptiveness. You'll start tapping into the wisdom which has been locked up tightly in your unconscious mind. When you tune-in to your full potential, you will be perceiving people and events through your unified-self programming rather than your separate-self programming.

As you continue to
uplevel your addictions to preferences,
you will increasingly
LOVE EVERYONE UNCONDITIONALLY—
INCLUDING YOURSELF.

Your love will no longer be a barter or
a business transaction in which you imply,
"I can love you if you fit my programming.
But if you don't, forget it.
I can't—or won't— love you."

"I'll love you **IF** . . ."
actually doesn't represent
genuine love at all.

When you begin to love EVERYONE
UNCONDITIONALLY—including yourself—
the people around you will begin to mirror
your loving energy and then love you
and cooperate with you in a way they
never could have done before.

When you try to force or manipulate people
into doing the things you want,
the most you get
is surface compliance or respect—
if you are lucky.
You can have respect for a person
and not feel love for him or her . . .
in fact, he or she may even fear you.

Your life won't work well
if people are afraid of you.

You can't trick them into loving you either.

It's love that gives maximum energy—
to you and to the people around you—
and this is the energy you really need
to make your life work well.

Loving people feel happy—
and happy people feel loving.

Please realize that it's only your programming
that blocks you from loving someone.

The only limit to your love
is the limit your programming puts on it!

"But how can I love my enemies?" you may ask.

Well, why are they "enemies"?

Only your programming makes you perceive
someone as an enemy.

Change your programming and
you can love everyone—UNCONDITIONALLY.
You can still be aware (and wary)
that perhaps their life games are not for you,
and maybe they're even for you to oppose.

Just don't throw them
out of your heart.

The best way to get rid of enemies
is to make them friends
in your own heart.
You can't afford to wait
for them to do it.

So now we see that
by upleveling addictions to preferences,
we begin to get the most
that's gettable in our lives.

We no longer louse up ourselves and others
by trying to get what is not gettable.

When we learn
to love people unconditionally,
we begin to experience
that life is a cornucopia
which offers us far more
security, sensations, and power
than we need to be happy.
When we don't demand
or anxiously anticipate ANYTHING—
EVERYTHING that comes along
can be appreciated and enjoyed to the fullest,
or emotionally accepted
as a present-moment part of life.

So how can we actually retrain our minds?

There are many great traditions
for reprogramming your biocomputer
and upleveling emotion-backed demands
into the preferences that can enable you
to flow with whatever
is here and now in your life.

The method we call "Living Love"
has been designed for us folks with big egos
and well-trained rational minds.

When you use these methods,
they help you get behind
your ego and rational mind
so that they become your faithful servants
rather than your master.

Whenever you feel upset
and are generating the experience of unhappiness,
it is because you are not following
one or more of
THE TWELVE LIVING LOVE PATHWAYS.

These PATHWAYS represent keys
to living a continuously happy,
fulfilled, loving life.

Not only do these PATHWAYS define
a marvelous set of goals to move toward . . .
they are, in themselves, an actual vehicle
for growing into your full potential.

They have thousands of years of wisdom
compressed into a small package
for instant use
whenever your separate-self programming
triggers feelings
of irritation, indignation, jealousy, worry,
disappointment, loneliness, etc.

When you find yourself rejecting
what's here and now in your life,
just tune-in to one of the PATHWAYS.

We recommend that you memorize
these PATHWAYS.

This will program them deeply into your
biocomputer so that you can begin
to use them automatically.

If you just read them over, they will remain
a shallow, intellectual thing that will not
get at the mainspring of the basic programming
which you now use to unconsciously trigger
separating emotions.

Simply "understanding" them is not enough.

Living Love requires that the TWELVE PATHWAYS
be PROGRAMMED deeply into your biocomputer
so that they replace the programming
which now automatically triggers unhappiness.

As you increase your use of these PATHWAYS . . .
you will experience growing energy, insight,
love, joy, and a feeling of purpose in your life!

There is no way
you can make yourself feel unhappy
unless you are violating one or more
of the TWELVE PATHWAYS.

Even physical pain
will not bring you unhappiness
as you increase your skill
in using the PATHWAYS!
(It will still hurt.)

Pain simply represents a physical sensation.

How you react to that sensation
is what causes unhappiness—
or emotional acceptance.

If you use the PATHWAYS,
you can more skillfully choose
your emotional reaction to the pain!

To repeat—
happiness depends
on emotional acceptance or rejection
in the here and now.
It does not depend on everything being
the way you want it to be.

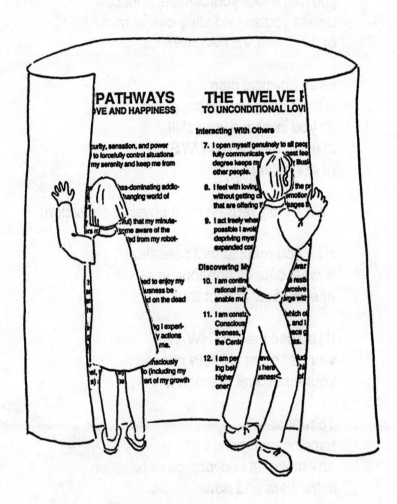

So here are the TWELVE PATHWAYS
that can help you free yourself
from programming which has been causing
unhappiness in your life . . . .

THE TWELVE PATHWAYS
TO UNCONDITIONAL LOVE AND HAPPINESS

Freeing Myself

1. I am freeing myself from security, sensation, and power addictions that make me try to forcefully control situations in my life, and thus destroy my serenity and keep me from loving myself and others.

2. I am discovering how my consciousness-dominating addictions create my illusory version of the changing world of people and situations around me.

3. I welcome the opportunity (even if painful) that my minute-to-minute experience offers me to become aware of the addictions I must reprogram to be liberated from my robot-like emotional patterns.

Being Here Now

4. I always remember that I have everything I need to enjoy my here and now—unless I am letting my consciousness be dominated by demands and expectations based on the dead past or the imagined future.

5. I take full responsibility here and now for everything I experience, for it is my own programming that creates my actions and also influences the reactions of people around me.

6. I accept myself completely here and now and consciously experience everything I feel, think, say, and do (including my emotion-backed addictions) as a necessary part of my growth into higher consciousness.

THE TWELVE PATHWAYS
TO UNCONDITIONAL LOVE AND HAPPINESS

Interacting With Others

7. I open myself genuinely to all people by being willing to fully communicate my deepest feelings, since hiding in any degree keeps me stuck in my illusion of separateness from other people.

8. I feel with loving compassion the problems of others without getting caught up emotionally in their predicaments that are offering them messages they need for their growth.

9. I act freely when I am tuned in, centered, and loving, but if possible I avoid acting when I am emotionally upset and depriving myself of the wisdom that flows from love and expanded consciousness.

Discovering My Conscious-awareness

10. I am continually calming the restless scanning of my rational mind in order to perceive the finer energies that enable me to unitively merge with everything around me.

11. I am constantly aware of which of the Seven Centers of Consciousness I am using, and I feel my energy, perceptiveness, love, and inner peace growing as I open all of the Centers of Consciousness.

12. I am perceiving everyone, including myself, as an awakening being who is here to claim his or her birthright to the higher consciousness planes of unconditional love and oneness.

THE TWELVE PATHWAYS
TO UNCONDITIONAL LOVE AND HAPPINESS

Freeing Myself

1. I am freeing myself from security, sensation, and power addictions that make me try to forcefully control situations in my life, and thus destroy my serenity and keep me from loving myself and others.

2. I am discovering how my consciousness-dominating addictions create my illusory version of the changing world of people and situations around me.

3. I welcome the opportunity (even if painful) that my minute-to-minute experience offers me to become aware of the addictions I must reprogram to be liberated from my robot-like emotional patterns.

Being Here Now

4. I always remember that I have everything I need to enjoy my here and now—unless I am letting my consciousness be dominated by demands and expectations based on the dead past or the imagined future.

5. I take full responsibility here and now for everything I experience, for it is my own programming that creates my actions and also influences the reactions of people around me.

6. I accept myself completely here and now and consciously experience everything I feel, think, say, and do (including my emotion-backed addictions) as a necessary part of my growth into higher consciousness.

THE TWELVE PATHWAYS
TO UNCONDITIONAL LOVE AND HAPPINESS

Interacting With Others

7. I open myself genuinely to all people by being willing to fully communicate my deepest feelings, since hiding in any degree keeps me stuck in my illusion of separateness from other people.

8. I feel with loving compassion the problems of others without getting caught up emotionally in their predicaments that are offering them messages they need for their growth.

9. I act freely when I am tuned in, centered, and loving, but if possible I avoid acting when I am emotionally upset and depriving myself of the wisdom that flows from love and expanded consciousness.

Discovering My Conscious-awareness

10. I am continually calming the restless scanning of my rational mind in order to perceive the finer energies that enable me to unitively merge with everything around me.

11. I am constantly aware of which of the Seven Centers of Consciousness I am using, and I feel my energy, perceptiveness, love, and inner peace growing as I open all of the Centers of Consciousness.

12. I am perceiving everyone, including myself, as an awakening being who is here to claim his or her birthright to the higher consciousness planes of unconditional love and oneness.

That may be a pretty big load
to pick up all at once—
although you probably understood
most of it quite well
INTELLECTUALLY.

You will have to live for a while
with the TWELVE PATHWAYS
to appreciate their deeper significances
and realize how they can affect
your moment-to-moment living.*

*The TWELVE PATHWAYS are explained in detail in *How to Enjoy Your Life in Spite of It All.* This easily understood, comprehensive book is written to help you make a real difference in your life. See page 202.

As you grow in awareness of how your mind works, you can observe the generators of thoughts, feelings, and actions we call the Seven Centers of Consciousness.

The first is the Security Center, followed by the Sensation Center and then the Power Center. These three centers can only produce a roller-coastering between emotional pleasure and emotional pain. When you are trapped in these three centers of consciousness, you are limited in the happiness you can create.

During the times when you're using preferential programming, you experience the happiness and unifying emotions of what we call the Fourth Center, or Love Center. The Fifth Center is known as the Cornucopia Center; here you experience the world as being like a horn of plenty which gives you more than you need to feel happy. Beyond that lies the Conscious-awareness Center and the exquisite Cosmic Consciousness Center.*

It is an incredibly beautiful experience to use the Centers of Consciousness as a frame of reference for watching yourself progress from a state of occasional pleasure to actually experiencing that happiness is increasingly becoming a part of your everyday life.

*More information on the Centers of Consciousness is available in *Handbook to Higher Consciousness*. See page 201.

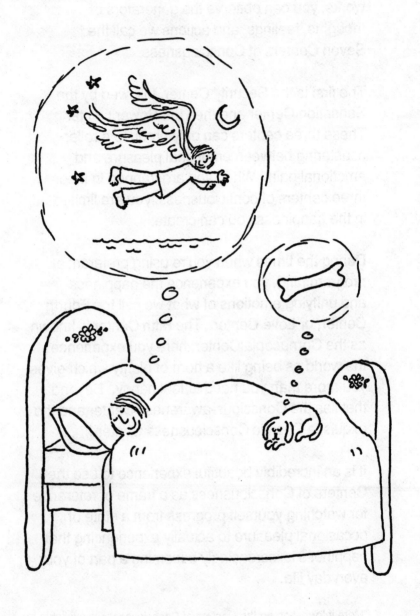

Man is an animal—a mammal.

Man, however, unlike any other animal, has a choice in using a "higher consciousness."

Generally, animals rely on their (1) security, (2) sensation, and (3) power programming. Some people spend most of their lives operating from these three Centers of Consciousness as well. But we can raise our consciousness to encompass (4) unconditional love; (5) deep appreciation of life; (6) a nonjudgmental perspective of it all; and (7) unity with the universe.

When we speak of using our "higher consciousness," we refer to the four higher centers that represent your and my full potential.

Without changing your outward activities, you may operate from Center 1, 2, 3, 4, 5, 6, or 7. Changing your center of consciousness involves modifying your inner motivations and perceptions—not necessarily changing the things you do.

Your present life activities can be much more fulfilling as you learn to use your higher centers more frequently and free yourself from all the demanding problems caused by the programs of the first three centers.

It has been said that this "secret" of happiness
cannot be taught—IT HAS TO BE CAUGHT!
Are you catching it?

It's here in this little book; but perhaps your
programming, your ego, and your rational mind
only let you understand a tiny part of it.

That's all right . . . that's the way it usually
happens. So just start reading the book again.
Really! Just turn back to the beginning and
start again . . . it's definitely worth it, you know.
After all, we're not just talking about myths
and fantasies . . . were talking about a key to
CONSISTENT HAPPINESS . . .
and this can be a REALITY for you!

No kidding! This book is telling you how you can
feel loving and happy more of the time.
There are lots of people DOING IT—RIGHT NOW.
Every time you read this book you may
understand a little bit more.

The FIRST THING that you can tune-in to
is an awareness of the connection between
your separating emotions and your
demanding programming.
ALL THE EMOTIONALLY UNPLEASANT
ASPECTS OF YOUR LIFE ARE CAUSED BY
ADDICTIONS YOU'VE PICKED UP SO FAR.
Is this becoming clearer?

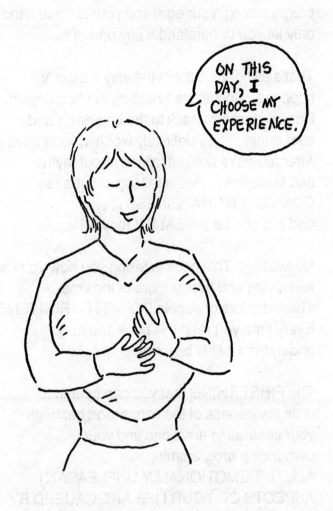

Your big breakthrough will come when you
CONSCIOUSLY EXPERIENCE that it is possible to uplevel an addiction to a preference.
This happens when you stop blaming
the outside world and see your demanding
programming as being the actual cause
of your turmoil.

Part of the "magical" experience that goes
along with this method is the realization that
you CAN reprogram your biocomputer.

In fact, YOU are the only one who can do it.

Consciousness growth can only come from your
deep inner motivation and commitment—
it cannot be imposed from the outside.

If you stumble . . . it's okay.

Just get up and go on.

DON'T BE ADDICTED TO NOT STUMBLING.

Have patience—set a goal to accept yourself
COMPLETELY just as you are—here and now.
(That's the SIXTH PATHWAY.)

If you have addictions here and now,
you have no choice but to accept them . . . .
Part of this method requires that you not
emotionally reject any aspect
of what is here and now.

Sure, you are trying to free yourself
from these addictions, but if they are part
of the here and now . . . what good will it do
to emotionally reject them—or yourself?

Simply make a conscious effort to experience
where you are at any given moment and get on
with the work of liberating yourself from the
addictions you are triggering here and now.

If you won't accept yourself just as you are,
you won't be able to accept and love
other people . . . unconditionally!

It takes time . . . and you've got the rest of
your life to do it.

Of course the faster you do it, the quicker
you can get off the roller-coastering between
emotional pleasure and emotional pain.

So let's get on with the inner work of
changing the programming that makes us
lock out of our hearts
the people and situations
that are here and now in our lives.

It is absolutely practical and possible
to create a consistently happy, loving,
conscious, fulfilled life.

When your understanding, determination,
and practical application of the methods
are strong and steady,
nothing will stop you
until you are there.

It is security, sensation, and power addictions
that are the germs which cause social
diseases: divorce, prejudice, economic
callousness, war, hatred, etc., etc., etc.

You can make an enormous contribution
toward solving the world's problems
(both group and individual).

JUST WORK ON YOUR OWN PROGRAMMING
so that you no longer spread
the addictive demands
that cause me-vs.-them separateness
throughout the world.

Don't get trapped in a separating habit of trying to preach to other people about how they should operate their consciousness. Just successfully demonstrate it in your own life. As you uplevel your demanding programming to preferential programming, by your own example you will be able to interest other people in getting rid of their addictions. Don't use Living Love as another means of trying to manipulate and control the human beings around you.

Remember, too, that ethnic groups, communities, and even nations have a consciousness. These large masses of people also act from security, sensation, and power centers. These group consciousnesses also have addictive programming. By working on yourself, you can start helping them move in an upward spiral which will ultimately raise the consciousness of all the world's societies.

Long ago it was written that "a journey of a thousand miles begins with a single step."

Reading this book is one more step.

When **you** love everyone and everything
in **your** life unconditionally, an inner light
will illuminate your hidden splendor.

People may come to you, open themselves,
and ask you to share with them how you
got rid of the disease called unhappiness.

Then, and only then, will you be able to
effectively explain that the germs which
cause the disease of unhappiness have been
identified as belonging to the species called
"addictus demandus."

Then you can furnish your friends with an
"antitoxin" known as the TWELVE PATHWAYS.

The TWELVE PATHWAYS may assist them
in building their body-mind-living love
immune systems.

Perhaps for the first time in your life
you will deeply experience
that you are playing a vital part in creating
the New Age of Humankind.

The more you use your "higher consciousness,"
the more you are helping to eliminate
the cause of human unhappiness.

So now you know how to make your life work.

You also know how to make your society work.

What are you going to do with this knowledge?

What will your present programming permit
you to do?

You've got answers to some of
the world's problems!

You know what you can do to live a more
deeply loving, conscious, fulfilled life.

You know how to help reduce
the rampant suffering
that is going on throughout the world,
so that coming generations
have a better chance
of making their lives work also.

You know how to transform your
inner programming so you can become
the creator of a New You and a New World.

You know how to experience
the wisdom, happiness, and fun in life
that is your birthright.

Life is an enjoyable game to be played—
not a horrendous problem to be solved.

When you uplevel your addictions to
preferences, thereby reducing your ego's
demands, you automatically increase your
power to create a heaven which you can
experience here and now on earth.

Saints and scholars have been saying this
in many ways through many ages . . . .

AND NOW
IT'S UP TO YOU!

Workshops for Personal Growth

Therapy is usually a costly and time-consuming process. It often involves hundreds of sessions at a cost of many thousands of dollars–over many years. Breakthrough methods that can produce rapid and effective healing of lifetraps are now being used. Ken Keyes Jr., a leader in the field of personal growth had been using a technique that he called "Caring Rapid Healing" (CRH) a healing program that usually heals childhood wounds in only five days.

The results with CRH have been phenomenal. It works directly with one's unconscious mind where the life-damaging injuries are locked in. The five days are focused on the *participant's particular requests for change.* CRH private workshops offer the opportunity to heal these "injuries" that are destroying relationships, tearing one's self esteem and one's confidence, and reducing fulfillment, aliveness, fun, inner peace, and happiness.

In a five day CRH private workshop, we work on one or more problem area chosen by the participant. Although most people find five days sufficient, sometimes more time may be required if one's problems are unusually complex and multilayered.

CRH is available to participants who are active, non-psychotic, drug free, and who can focus their energy into healing their false-self injuries so that they can enjoy their lives.

We are also in the process of developing a process that directly addresses drug and alcohol, as well as other addictions.

For more information contact:
CRH Registration
The Ken Keyes Institute of Higher Consciousness
In care of Love Line Books
800-E Fairview Road #269
Asheville, NC 28803
or call toll free 1-800-976-8312
Or visit our web sight at http://www.livinglove.org

Ken passed away on December 20, 1995 and he will be missed by all of us. Since his passing I have been working to find and train someone whom I felt could do the work that Ken was doing and someone who would be loved as much as Ken was loved. In mid 1996 I found Jamie Black. Jamie is what I consider to be a natural born healer. She has been trained in most of the facets of healing that Ken used as well as a few more that we thought would go well with the healing techniques that Ken used. I think that she is going to make a wonderful addition to our family.

You might be wondering who I am. Please, let me introduce myself. I am Guy Menadier, President of the Living Love Church (founded by Ken in 1972) and Love Line Books. I knew Ken for 32 years. He inspired me even before he started on his journey to Higher Consciousness. I had been working for and living with Ken for about three years when he passed away. The Board of Directors of the Living Love Church asked me to handle all of the daily ongoing business of the company until they could figure out what to do. The Board thought that it would be best to dissolve the corporation but I pleaded with them to let me try to continue with Ken's work. After everything was said and done I was elected President of the corporation and told by the Board of Directors to try to continue with Ken's work, but at all costs, to continue to get Ken's books out to the world.

This is the first reprint of this book since Ken's passing. We are getting ready to move to North Carolina and I hope that we will be able to offer workshops by about mid summer 1997. We will continue to reprint Ken's books as needed and hopefully I can make this business continue to work as well as Ken did.

With Living Love,
Guy

For more information about the workshops by Jamie Black and other trainers please contact us at:

The Ken Keyes Institute of Higher Consciousness
In care of Love Line Books
800-E Fairview Road #269
Asheville, NC 28803
or call toll free 1-800-976-8312

Books by Ken

Handbook to Higher Consciousness
Ken Keyes, Jr., $9.95

Why are our lives filled with turmoil and worry? Why do we allow ourselves only small dribbles of peace, love, and happiness? *Handbook to Higher Consciousness* presents practical methods that can help you create happiness and unconditional love in your life. Countless people have experienced a dramatic change in their lives from the time they began applying the effective techniques explained in the *Handbook*. There are over one million in print worldwide.

Handbook to Higher Consciousness The Workbook
Ken Keyes, Jr. and Penny Keyes, $8.95

Filled with three months of worksheets, this workbook is geared for the busy person. In 15 to 20 minutes a day, you can begin to apply the methods presented in the *Handbook to Higher Consciousness* in your day-to-day interactions with yourself and others. Each day you are gently guided to uncover those roadblocks that are keeping you from experiencing the most joyful life possible. Based on years of practice by thousands of "living lovers," this workbook offers an essential step into higher consciousness.

Gathering Power Through Insight and Love
Ken Keyes, Jr., and Penny Keyes, $9.95

Here's how to do it! This outstanding book gives you detailed instructions on exactly how to develop the love inside you. It describes the 2-4-4 system for going from the separate-self to the unified-self: 2 Wisdom Principles, 4 Living Love Methods, and 4 Dynamic Processes. This book is based on our years of leading workshops. These skills are essential for those who want the most rapid rate of personal growth using the Science of Happiness.

How to Enjoy Your Life in Spite of It All
Ken Keyes, Jr., $10.95

Learn to enjoy your life no matter what others say or do! The Twelve Pathways explained in this book are a modern, practical condensation of thousands of years of accumulated wisdom. Using these proven pathways will help you change your thoughts from separating, automatic reactions to practical, loving ways of thinking. They promote deep levels of insight, and help bring increased energy, inner peace, love, and perceptiveness into your moment-to-moment living. A must for people who are sincerely interested in their personal growth.

Discovering the Secrets of Happiness: My Intimate Story
Ken Keyes, Jr., $9.95

In this inspiring story, Ken shares his own journey of inner growth from an unfulfilled man seeking happiness through sex and money to a respected teacher of personal growth and world peace. Ken candidly expresses his successes and failures as he recounts how he gave up a lucrative business grossing $32 million dollars a year to dedicate his life to serving others, and how he has harnessed the power of "super love" to create a deeply fulfilling marriage with his wife, Penny. He he tells how you can enormously benefit from applying the secrets he discovered.

Prescriptions for Happiness
Ken Keyes, Jr., $7.95

Use these easy-to-remember secrets for happiness. Works for both children and adults. Designed for busy people, this book can be absorbed in about an hour. These simple prescriptions work wonders. They help you put more fun and aliveness into your interactions with people. Learn to ask for what you want with love in your heart. Benefit from techniques that boost insight, love, and enjoyment in our uncertain world. Some people, after reading this book, buy out the bookstore and give copies to their friends. 159,000 in print.

Your Heart's Desire—
A Loving Relationship
Ken Keyes, Jr., $7.95

Do you want to bring the magic of enduring love into your relationship? All of us have had a taste of what heart-to-heart love is like. We cherish those times and strive to experience them continuously. Using your rich inner resources, this book can inspire you to create a more loving relationship—without your partner having to change! It can help you to beautifully deepen the harmony, love, empathy, and trust in your relationship.

The Power of
Unconditional Love:
21 Guidelines for Beginning, Improving, and Changing Your Most Meaningful Relationships
Ken Keyes, Jr., $10.95

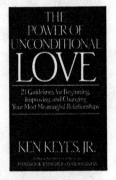

A complete revision of the popular classic *A Conscious Person's Guide to Relationships.*

➤ You are shown how the enormous of power of unconditional love can enable you to create a wonderful trust and comfort with the diverse issues, different backgrounds, and changing wants and interests of your loved ones.

➤ It contains guidelines to help you prepare yourself for a relationship that can fulfill your heart's desire for love and intimacy.

➤ It explains additional guidelines that can make your relationship richer and more delightful.

➤ And it also offers guidelines for how you can let go of a relationship with love and wisdom.

The Hundredth Monkey
Ken Keyes, Jr., Pocketbook, $5.95

There is no cure for nuclear war—ONLY PREVENTION! This book shows you that we have the creativity and power to change both ourselves and the world. You are introduced to a radical new way of realizing the impact of your energy on the world around you—a quantum leap in consciousness. You'll find here the facts about our nuclear predicament that some people don't want you to know. Internationally acclaimed, over one million copies have been distributed throughout the world. This dynamic little book has been translated into nine languages, including Russian.

PlanetHood
Benjamin B. Ferencz and Ken Keyes, Jr., Pocketbook, $7.95

This breakthrough book, which is the sequel to *The Hundredth Monkey*, explains how you can personally give yourself and your family a future in this nuclear age. It tells how we can replace the *law of force* with the *force of law*. It explains eight ways you can personally help the world settle disputes *legally*—instead of *lethally*! We are making *PlanetHood* available on a nonprofit basis. The list price of *PlanetHood* is $2.50. For only $3 postpaid, we will mail a copy of this book to any person in the world for whom you furnish the name and address. If you buy a case of 100, we will mail the case anywhere in the United States at a cost of only 70¢ per book (a total of $70 postpaid in the U.S.). If you buy 1,000 or more, they will cost only 50¢ per book (a total of $500 including shipping in the U.S.).

All these books are available in bookstores
or see pages 208-209 for ordering information.

Two powerful workshops on tape!

Handbook to Higher Consciousness

Ken Keyes, Jr.

$9.95, Cassette
approximately 1 hour

Includes a
32-page Mini-Guide to
Higher Consciousness

➤ One of the most charismatic and acclaimed philosophers of the New Age, Ken personally brings to you on audiotape his modern, practical blueprint for a life of love and happiness.

➤ Includes a 32-page Mini-Guide to Higher Consciousness that can guide you toward a vibrant, loving, happy, and fulfilled life!

➤ If you've had enough of the up-and-down roller-coastering between pleasure and pain, then you are ready to use and apply these step-by-step methods to improve your life while you live it!

Gathering Power Through Insight and Love

Ken and Penny Keyes

$15.95, 2 Cassettes

Includes a
48-page Workbook

➤ These dynamic cassettes are taken from the popular workshops designed by Ken and Penny Keyes.

➤ Expanding on the principles found in the *Handbook*, Ken and Penny explain and demonstrate specific techniques that can help you put the Living Love methods to work daily.

➤ Offers practical and precise ways to develop the skills for radically improving the quality of your life.

206

ORDERING INFORMATION

Books

$19.95	Your Road Map To Lifelong Happiness
$9.95	Handbook to Higher Consciousness
$8.95	Handbook to Higher Consciousness: The Workbook
$9.95	Discovering the Secrets of Happiness: My Intimate Story
$9.95	Gathering Power Through Insight and Love
$10.95	How to Enjoy Your Life in Spite of It All
$7.95	Prescriptions for Happiness
$7.95	Your Heart's Desire
$5.95	The Hundredth Monkey
$7.95	PlanetHood

Audio Cassettes

$9.95	Handbook to Higher Consciousness, with a 32-page Mini-Guide
$15.95	Gathering Power Through Insight and Love, two tapes with a 48-page workbook

For a price list of all books written by Ken Keyes Jr. please write to: Love Line Books, 700 Commercial Ave., Coos Bay, OR 97420-1747 or call 541-269-2812 from 9:00 a.m. to 5:00 p.m. Pacific Time.

TO ORDER BOOKS AND TAPES

Qty.	Item No.	Item	Price	Amount

Please include shipping charges:
$3.00 first item, $1.00 for each additional item

Subtotal
Shipping
TOTAL

☐ **Yes!** Please put me on your mailing list and send me a free catalog listing workshops, books, posters, music albums and cassettes, and audio and video tapes.

Ship to: (please print) _____

Address _____

City _____

State _____ Zip _____

Telephone No. ( ) _____

For ( ) VISA or ( ) MasterCard orders only:
Card # _____

Exp. Date _____ Signature: _____

Ken Keyes' books may be purchased through any bookstore. For mail order, send you check in U.S. funds or credit card information to Love Line Books, 700 Commercial Avenue, Coos Bay, OR 97420. To order by phone with VISA or Master Card call: (541) 269-2812, Monday through Friday, 9:00 a.m. to 4:30 p.m. Pacific time.